The Heart That Beats

2010 – 2016

Czech Republic and California

Hans Joseph Fellmann

WingSpan Press

Published in the United States and the United Kingdom by WingSpan Press, Livermore, CA

The WingSpan name, logo and colophon are the trademarks of WingSpan Publishing.

ISBN 978-1-59594-651-5 (pbk.)
ISBN 978-1-59594-963-9 (ebk.)

First edition 2020

Printed in the United States of America

www.wingspanpress.com

Library of Congress Control Number: 2020911365

1 2 3 4 5 6 7 8 9 10

For my mother:
The voice of goodness in my terribly fucked-up head.

Author's Note

This collection of poems documents my life as a novice writer living in the Czech Republic and California from 2010 to 2016. All poems appear in chronological order. Names, locations, descriptions, and scenes have been altered or changed completely to protect the identities of those involved and to suit the flow of the narrative.

Contents

I could write a devastating poem
One which slits open the underbelly
of society, spilling its innards
across the stage
for the world to see.
But it would not matter.
The morons would still
flourish
The murderers would still
murder
And the teenybopper
with her cherry lipstick
would still suck the cocks
of a thousand false gods.
So fuck it
I'm gonna do this for me.
And when the worms
eat through
my molded corpse
they'll finish on
a nice big smile.

A Knowing Smile

I see my reflection in the mirror

and smile at it

Something inside calls to me

I glide my hand forward

My fingers touch the glass

which ripples as they sink in

The feeling is pleasant

at first

But then, I am yanked

into my own reflection

My forearm, my elbow, my shoulder, my torso

Liquid glass floods my screaming mouth

I feel a snap.

Then weightlessness

I am floating in space

Stars are all around me

I reach for one

Its gravity pulls me

like a bullet shot through jelly.

Faster and faster I go

from body to board to blade

I am a speeding beam of light, slicing infinity apart with shivering fingers

I hurtle toward a fiery planet

orbiting the star

I rush through its red membranes

and touch down to the ground

Death is already there, waiting for me.

He takes my hand with his slow skeletal grip and leads me
through the light

We weave past rivers of fire so bright my pupils are turned to
pinpricks

We come to a crack in a white mountain and he ushers me inside
where a blue corridor stretches on forever

We walk for what seems like days
as our echoing footsteps melt into nothingness

My eyelids begin to hang

But as I touch the brink of sleep

I feel a snap.

I am awake and before me is a tall throne
where the Man himself sits

His gaze makes me kneel

"What is all this?" I ask

"You tell me," he says

I look up at him and he smiles

So I smile back.

I feel the pull again

This time I roll with it

I am sucked toward the center of his forehead

at the moment of touch, needles of light expand in every direction.

I tumble back through the mirror and land on two feet.

I see my reflection

then look down at my hands and say to myself

"Pull the blade away from your wrist."

Dog Days

Outside my window, there are dogs that bark
But from the fifth floor, I can't very well step out
To hush them. So I must tolerate the noise.
Hell, if the halo of crummy buildings didn't amplify the sound
Things might not be so bad. You see,
Sometimes, the barking wakes me up in the morning.
Other times, the barking starts
Right as I lay down to sleep or sit down to write.
Most times, the barking carries on for twenty minutes or more.
It comes from different dogs, each armed with different barks,
Some are low and threatening like the boom of a subwoofer,
Some are high and creaky like an unoiled door hinge,
Some whine and whine like a spoiled brat in the back seat,
And some grind my guts and make me want to murder.
Then the fantasies creep into my thoughts.
Sniping the little shit's head from my window
Is a popular one.
Walking outside in boxers and clubbing the mutt to a meaty pulp
with a crowbar
Is another.
Approaching the pooch with a smile and feeding it rat poison
From the palm of my hand definitely makes the list.
I even fantasize about fucking the little mongrel,
Making sure his pea-brain gets the hint.
You might be wondering

Hans Joseph Fellmann

Why the violence? Why

The frequency? Why do all the different dogs bark?

Well, outside my window is a grocery store,

And outside the store is a fenced-in den,

Some people who come to this grocery store are lazy

Idiots, who figure they'll get their dog-walking and shopping done

In the same huff. So, they tie their dogs up

At the den and walk in the store

Then the dogs get lonely

And they start to bark.

I'd say I feel bad for the buggers, especially in this heat,

But I don't.

I just want them to die.

So I can finally get some peace.

POS

I hate my bed.
It is a piece of shit
Not just uncomfortable
No, its shittiness stretches far beyond discomfort
Allow me to explain

First, the flimsy wooden grate isn't fixed in place
Whenever I move, each individual board shifts
In a different direction. When one shifts too far
It slips from the frame and pops
Down. But not all the way to the ground
It's still connected to every other board by a sticky rope of sorts
It hangs there, lifelessly
So, the mattress above no longer receives any support.
This creates a depression, which, if left unattended
Causes nearby boards to fall loose from the frame.
This deepens the depression.

Once, while I was having sex, a board popped away from the frame.
I tried to ignore it
But as the stripper bounced up and down on my cock, another
board popped free.
Then another, then another, then another.
Soon, a heavy ripping sound filled the air,
Half the bed gave way beneath us

We crashed to the ground in a heap of sweaty flesh

The stripper laughed

I screamed.

See, during the fall, my cock was only halfway in

At a weird angle

So, when we landed

It bent

In half.

The pain caused my bowels to loosen

Right there, on the damn mattress.

So, there I was

there *we* were

In a pile of shit.

On a pile of shit.

Bad Onion

My roommate is an odd one.
He comes in late,
Stinking of cheese and feet,
Cheap cologne and sausage,
Says ciao in that creepy way
With too many front teeth.
He wears dinner jackets to clubs,
Flip-flops to work,
And glasses
Even though he doesn't need to.
He rocks when he talks
And cheats strangers without flinching
An affable chap.
But like a bad onion, he's
Sweet then sour,
 Sweet then sour.
Sometimes I want to shank him in the belly.
 Sometimes I want to thank him for the jelly.
Sometimes
I even get the feeling
He's a queer.
But just when this reaches its peak
He brings home a 300-pound gypsy whore
And fucks her in the bathroom.
I can't stand the guy

Hans Joseph Fellmann

Really

I can't

Especially when he leaves his unwashed dishes

Stacked in the sink

Like a porcelain shipwreck.

I've come close to killing him

A time or two

But then he gives me a slice of bacon

Or a restaurant tip

And things are okay

Again, for a bit.

Thanks for Sharing

Last night, a friend was honest.
After reading my poetry
she told me that it was
raw but not quite *there.*
Not yet.
Her tone was delicately condescending
like an adult talking
to a slow child.
"Thanks for sharing," she said.
This type of response I'd expect
from a Mervyn's catalogue
after sending in my opinion
on a pair of undies.
Did she know what I've sacrificed?
My health,
My youth,
My family,
A child?
Life is passing me by.
And all I hear are those
three miserable words

Enlightenment

I'm so tired

I want to sleep

I must write something first

But this beast is so fickle

Why can't I put things down on paper exactly when I want to?

Why must I constantly be at the whim of my internal mechanisms?

Don't I have any say in the matter?

I am, after all, me.

Shouldn't that mean that every part of me is mine to control?

If not, which parts of me can be considered "me" and which parts not?

And at what point, if parts were removed, do I stop being "me"?

Is there a line that can be drawn between what's "you" and what's not "you" within "you"?

If not, then what exactly are "you"?

What exactly is "I"?

Maybe "I" is everything within "you," only some parts of that whole are inaccessible until proper enlightenment is achieved?

Maybe enlightenment is a scam dreamed up by haughty bearded men who know what we all fear?

Maybe I'm just thinking too hard?

Maybe thinking is the wrench that blocks the gears of enlightenment from spinning?

I don't know,

But it's now sunrise,

The Heart That Beats

and the light is

hurting my

eyes

The Heart That Beats

Is there a heart that beats
beneath it all?

Past the heaps of natives,
    smoking and wrinkled.
Past the heads of slaves,
    hanging and swollen.
Past the bodies of soldiers,
    grey and blue.
Past the cannon fire,
    the tank shells,
    And the rocket blasts?

Is there a heart that beats
beneath it all?

Past the hunted immigrants
    and the barbed-wire fences.
Past the filthy slums
    and the decadent suburbs.
Past the drone-screen killings
    and the in-vogue wars.
Past the scandals,
    the corruption,
    and the lies?

The Heart That Beats

Is there a heart that beats
beneath it all?

Past the hordes of celebrities,
    paid in limbs.
Past the wards of doctors
    charging the same.
Past the packs of lawyers
    harvesting the rest.
Past the pimps,
    the pushers,
    and the prostitutes?

Is there a heart that beats
beneath it all?

Past the red 'n white stripes
    and the fifty proud stars.
Flapping at a sky
    that was never ours,
Past the shopping mall sales
    and the school shootouts,
Past the serial,
    the political,
    and the subliminal murder?

Is there a heart that beats
    beneath it all?

Past the sweeping oil spills
    and the deforestation.
Past the three-headed chickens
    and the pink-slime meat.
Past the towering smog clouds
    and the caustic rain,
Past the sewage,
    the sludge,
    and the radiation?

Is there a heart that beats
beneath it all?
And, if so, what does it look like?

Like a Coke can?
Like a Big Mac?
Like a corn chip?
Like a laptop?
Like a cheap car?
Like a flat beer?
Like a pop star?
Like a sitcom?

I put my hand across my chest and hope
with bated breath
But all I get
are fingers, waiting.
    Fingers, waiting.
    Fingers, waiting.

Czech

Czech is

Crystal chewed
by steel teeth

A stream of Uzi bullets
whizzing through snowfall

A ballerina
weaving effortlessly
through a tangle of barbed wire

Death, sat still
on a throne of ice

Winter's breath glistening
along crooked branches

The neatly splintered madness
of a pondering mathematician

A sea urchin stuck
in the foot of a dumb American

Yet past its spines,

Hans Joseph Fellmann

those towering black spires,
lay little lobes of yellow
nestled together
shining
For no one to see.

A Spic like Me

When I was a kid
I chilled with my gramps
He was an old school spic
With tequila in his veins
And white hair
He used to walk me to the moon on his shoulders
Telling stories
Of Juarez bootleggers
El Paso murders
And pretty girls
With roses for ears.
He spoke Spanish
I did too
He spread chili on his pancakes
I did too
At the breakfast table
We sat
Six and sixty-six
Sipping near beer
And cracking dirty jokes
I was his "Muchacho Alegre."

At the schoolyard
that all changed
Kids saw my tan skin

Hans Joseph Fellmann

heard my accent

They asked my name

"Why, it's Johann Klaus Felmanstien," I said. "Y qué?"

The gravel turned hot with laughter

"Johann?" they said

"But don't you speak Spanish? I mean, what kinda spic are you?"

I asked my daddy that night

His belly rolled

and his beard lit up as he said

"The kind with a German name."

After that, I started seeing things like

Nazis in my bedroom

Smoking cigarettes

Einstein's face in my cereal bowl

When I hit the piñata

It burst into sauerkraut

When I sipped my horchata

It turned into schnapps

I walked around the playground

Like a freak on stilts

Poncho on one shoulder

Lederhosen strap on the other

One day

While getting lit into

I made a friend

He was a black kid

A "nigger," like me

The Heart That Beats

He told me, "Stiffen up. Don't let 'em call you spic.'"

I said, "Thanks for that."

He said, "No problem, my nigga."

From then on, I walked wit a limp,

Put candy in my grin

And braided my hair,

When fools tried to test me

I showed 'em a nigga pimp,

Slapped 'em across the jaw,

Made they face raw,

But still I couldn't shake 'em,

I was more a spic than ever,

Glidin' up the block

Wit zebra painted skin,

I tried to hide in others

But nothing seemed to work

The Asians saw a Persian

The Persians saw a Turk

When all was lost

I grabbed a bottle

Put it to my lips

And chugged

What came out

Was puke, piss, and shit

After that

Came words

I put them on the page

To sew myself together

Hans Joseph Fellmann

Now I sit before you

Reading what I wrote

You see the tan

You see the skin

You see the kraut

You see the grin

The pimp, the clothes

The limp, the nose.

All tacked together

A sombrero at my back

Homie,

You ain't never seen a spic like me.

Pavlina's Wolf

Pavlina,

You were good to me
When I was a prick.
You cooked for me
And nursed me back to health
When my liver was swollen
And my voice was gone.

I remember our sunny days
And our walks through the park
You tried to hold my hand
But I kept it in my pocket.
It's not that I don't care for you
I do
So much that I cry at night.
Sometimes I sit at my desk
And let it all out
The tears slide down my cheeks
And into my mouth.

I feel like a shit
because I won't love you.
I'm scared, you see
Scared I'll disappoint you
and myself.

Hans Joseph Fellmann

I know I have a wandering eye
It moves over so many women

You told me I was a wolf
You were right

To the Writer in the Room

Do everything the opposite.
While they start their cars,
You tie your shoes.
While they work their jobs,
You walk your streets.
While they end their night,
You grab your pen.
And while they sleep,
You write.
Till your eyes ache,
till your bones crack,
till your fingers bleed.
Then,
while the sun rises,
and they sip their lattes,
you swig your whiskey
and dance with the whores.

Back Home Again

My sister and I snaked our way up the 405
As John Denver's sweet country voice
Bled through the speakers
My sister nodded and sang along
I just folded my arms and grinned
"Wanna know what this song makes me think of?"
I asked. My sister thinned her lips
"Hmm."
"It makes me think," I said,
"of two ballsacks swinging and jiggling while two dick-tips kiss
beneath the eave of a shitty asshole."
Her eyes widened
      her nostrils flared
"Johann," she told me. "You just took a *coot* little song,
And turned it into an absolutely disgusting pornographic image,"
I laughed out loud as
good ol' Johnny belted out the chorus,
Boy, was he right.

Two and Thirty

As we drove down PCH last Saturday
the traffic lay out
like a cosmic python
stretching, hissing
for miles and miles
as the sun above
made its scales glitter.

Our dog was in the back,
    her breath reeking of fish.
My father was up front
    his head an angry block of ham.
He slammed the horn
and cursed the traffic.
"These pauses are a fuckin' illusion," he barked,
"Two seconds of excitement and thirty minutes of misery."
My mom sat back.
She shrugged.
"Such is life."

The Mason

When the night buries
its claws in me
and tears the flesh from
my bones
I get a poem

When the skeleton winks
from the rocking boat
and I feel myself
being dragged down
I get a poem

When the blinds become
long teeth
loose in their gums
and the maggots pour
in through the gaps
I get a poem

When the clock melts
from its nail
and I'm left
crying on the floor
with numbers stuck to my fingers
I get a poem

The Heart That Beats

When the phone rings
and I pick it up
cool as a blue jay, only
to hear a gunshot
down the line
I get a poem

For every tear
I get a letter

For every scream
I get a word

One day I'll be a broken man haunting
a castle of books

Mattie of Shell Beach

We drove by a low sitting mansion on Ocean BLVD,

Its backside hung off a cliff

And its brown façade bore

Big white teeth

And the number

1029

"That house is famous," said my Dad's buddy Jim

"Why's that?" I asked

"Because, it's the former home of Mattie. She used to run a
bordello up the way that doubled as a tavern. Back in the 50s
and 60s, all the sailors would go up there, get drunk then seek
other entertainment. Mattie took care of 'em all. She was a local
celebrity. In fact, when she wasn't running the tavern, she'd throw
wild parties at this house with all the artists and millionaires and
politicians in the area, even brought down her girls sometimes to
fluff the company. Legends of these shindigs spread all throughout
SLO County. Since my family knew Mattie, a few of her stories even
made it to my ears."

"Really? What kinda stories?"

"Oh, nothing too juicy. I was just a kid when I met her. And by the
time I was old enough to hear anything worthwhile, the murder
happened."

"Murder?"

"Yeah, a couple'a hippie types broke into her house while she was
up working the tavern. They found her husband Edgar inside alone

and shot him a buncha times in the face. Cops caught the guys forty-eight hours later, even convicted 'em, but that didn't matter. Mattie was a wreck. After that, everything just sorta crumbled."

"Jesus, that's sad. Do people around here still know of her?"

"Older generation may, but all the young ones are clueless. Her tavern is now named F. McLintock's and her house has different owners."

"Any trace of her left?" I asked. "In Shell Beach, I mean."

Jim pointed. "That's pretty much it."

Out the window
On the side of the road
I read the word "Mattie"
In faded print on an
Old street sign.

Sasquatch

One sunny day in August
I met my friends Don and Dave
On a beach in SF,
We walked onto the sand
With blankets and towels
And set up shop
Five meters from the water

Dave got on the phone
Called some friends
Who showed up an hour later
With umbrellas, chairs, drinks, and food
All yuppie types
Box-cut glasses
Big rich smiles,
They crowded around our little space,
Cracking beers and jokes,
Laughing and yelling,
I got quiet and stared at my hairy toes,
Dave asked me what was up,
"I'm just thinking," I said,
He opened his mouth
And his teeth glinted
"About what?" he asked,
I shrugged and slid my eyes to one side,

The Heart That Beats

"Like what if a bum popped a squat over a gutter

And you cupped your hands under his ass

And washed them with his diarrhea?"

Don choked on his beer,

Dave's face reddened,

"Johann talks like this," he said, apologizing to the yuppies,

A girl named Tara with

Blond streaks and buck teeth

Raised an eyebrow,

"I'm not gonna lie," she said,

"That was fucking disgusting, but a pretty vivid image.

Can you do another one?"

The crowd shrunk around me,

I grunted and

Sat up straight,

"Okay Tara," I said,

"What if you saw a skeleton of veins

Playing hopscotch across the beach?"

She kicked her chin up and cackled,

Then another yuppie,

Who'd been swimming,

Walked up,

"Rob," Tara said to him. "What if you saw a skeleton

Of veins playing hopscotch on the beach?"

Rob furrowed his brow,

"Why?" he asked, "Did you guys just see someone super anorexic?"

Dave slapped the sand, "Oooooh, that was a good answer, Johann,"

he said,

"You're gonna hafta hit him with another."
Rob still looked confused,
I narrowed my eyes,
"So Rob," I said. "What if sasquatch sprung from a cloud and did a
cannonball directly into your eye socket?"
His face turned waxy
As he processed the image,
"What the fuck?" he said, giggling,
This provoked all the yuppies to
Ask me what-if's,
I pointed around the group
And posed questions like:

"What if you opened your underwear drawer
And a woman screamed?"

"What if you were eating hot soup and your
Teeth turned to butter and
Melted from your gums?"

"What if you pulled my finger and it
Popped from my knuckle
Into a bouquet of flowers?"

"What if you dropped your pants and
Your legs weren't there?"

"Or how 'bout if I told you that you looked like
Two hands clapping in the dark?

Or schizophrenic apples?
Or wobbly knees down steps?
Or ashes sword-fighting?"

This went on and on,
While they laughed
I absconded
To a nearby latrine,
Over my shoulder, I heard Tara say,
"What if we could pick apart those
Questions he asked and find out
Something about Johann?"
 "What if?" I thought

Gestapo Princess

On the playground of lunatics
I was alone without a muse,
I searched for her in
Whorehouses and dive bars,
Moonlit fields and building shells,
I tried for her with alcohol and mad fungus,
Strange pills and tea leaves,
When she didn't come
I dropped to my knees,
Cupped my hands
And begged.
"Please, dear spirits," I said. "Send me a lady
To prick my fingers and warm my head."
I waited in vain for years on end,
And while others got kisses
And wet their pens,
I got a big fat
nothing.

Then one day,
While I was toying with a razorblade,
A woman entered my room,
She was tall and hunched
With one broken shoe,
Rancid-milk arms

The Heart That Beats

And a dead-flower dress,
She ticked with the clap
Of boots on skulls,
Her mouth was a cage of fire,
Her eyes were smiling bullet holes,
I asked for her name
    and she said it was "Hilda,"
I asked for her business
    and she pulled out a gun.

Before I could react,
She jammed it up my ass,
Slammed me to the keyboard
And told me,
"Get crackin'"

I jerked and kicked
    tried to escape
But as I did, she fired.
The bullet ripped through my organs
And into my brain,
Popped out the top
And made my blood rain.

Before I knew it,
The pages were soaked,
Dripping with letters
And pieces of me.

Hans Joseph Fellmann

It was then that I knew
I'd been granted my wish,
My luger maiden
My Gestapo Princess

End Scene

Sometimes I get low,
Real low,
So far bottom that the top
becomes a microscopic pinprick
In a sea of blackness
And my eyes are the
Saddest little scabs
Looking up at it.
When this happens,
All good things
Fade

The locks of a woman's hair
Turn to spider legs
The flowers hang from their pots
Like wet socks
The moon in the sky
Becomes a staple
The smile on my mother's face
Crumbles to ash

I kneel at the toilet
With my lips touching
The smelly water,
I wretch and

Hans Joseph Fellmann

God becomes a bucket of fish guts
And Jesus, a three-dollar
Blowjob

I retire to my room and pour a drink
And while the dogs go rabid
And surround my building,
And the cats turn feral
And hiss through
Their fangs,
The ice cubes
In my glass
Clink quietly
And the liquid
Curtain slowly
Closes

A Better Place

Last Friday, in a Žižkov dive bar
With driftwood tables and floors
Covered in cigarette butts,
I ordered a drink from the fat barmaid
And struck up a chat with some dude
Whose face was so freckled
I could barely see
His eyes. We got on the topic
Of writing and he asked me
Why.

"I wanna make the world a better place," I said,
He poured beer down his throat and laughed,
"How the fuck are you gonna do that
By sitting at your desk and typing all day?"

My fingers curled,
I wanted to take the bottle from his hand
And smash it over his head,
Then I wanted to stomp
The glass into his freckly face
While he screamed on the ground and bled out.
Instead, I went home and wrote this poem,
I showed it to him the next day
And bought him a beer.

Being Away

After many months abroad,
I sit in my backyard
Drinking coffee, I look around and notice,
That the oranges have lost their green,
The roses have lost their petals,
The patio has lost its sheen,
And the red tree
That used to remind me
Of an exploding wall of blood
Has been reduced to
A few stick-fingers
Behind the fence.

I've been away for a long time.
Soon, I will
leave again.

Just Kidding

"If murder was legal,
There would be so much murder."

Louis C.K. was right, I think.

See, today, when I went to that dungeon

Of sheetrock and fluorescent lights

They call "Cizinecká policie" or

The Foreign Police, I was expecting

to receive my two-year visa.

Back in September, I had applied.

But when I got to the window, I was told

By a lady with plastic curls

And a red-painted mouth

That due to a lack of health insurance,

My stay had been shortened to a year.

"Are you serious?"

"Of course, Mr. Felmanstien," she replied,

"You gave us insurance valid only for a year."

"No way," I said, "I bought insurance

valid for two years. Check my file."

She picked through my papers

with the tips of her acrylic nails,

found my insurance details,

and flapped them in front of her glasses.

Hans Joseph Fellmann

"See," she said, pointing,
"It says 'one year.'"
"Not possible," I said, "I'm certain
I gave you two years' worth."

"It's not in your file," she assured me,
"So, you'll have to go
through the whole process again
next September."

As she sat there, shuffling papers and scribbling nonsense,
I wanted to reach out and wrap my fingers around her neck
Then when she opened her yap, I wanted to choke a scream out of it
And strangle her till the makeup on her cheeks cracked
and the veins on her temples
Burst.
Once she was dead, I would cheer
    and shout and stand on her desk.
Open my fly and piss straight in
    her mouth.

When my murderous reverie ended,
She handed me my visa.
I took it with a precious smile
And walked out, thinking about
What Louis said.
If only it was legal.

Go Franta

Franta is the office rebel,
who sports black leather vests and holey jeans
He wears his Mohawk short and, from his left ear,
He hangs a tiny silver skull.
During workdays,
He high-fives his colleagues and types between smoke breaks.
On weekends,
He jams with his band, drinks Pilsner, and flashes the devil horns,
And every now and then,
He bends his blond wife over the kitchen sink
And eats her ass.
When Monday drops,
He's hungover and reeking of beer,
But he shows up at the office on time and, boy,
Does he bring the laughs.
Everybody loves Franta as he spouts off tales
Of poolside drunkenness and cool garage concerts,
Suburban street mayhem and urinating in the woods,
People bring him coffee
And pat him on the back,
Though no one ever
Looks him in
The eyes.

City Slickin'

While hungover on the couch
One Saturday morning
My friend Bert and I
Had a breakthrough.
We came up with something called
"City Slickin'"
Which even the mere thought of brought tears
To our eyes and made us laugh
So hard we almost threw up
Our Friday-night kebabs.
For the rest of the day,
We went around
telling each other to "City Slick"
so-and-so.
Fat guy on a bench?
    City Slick 'em,
Old dude in the park?
    City Slick 'em,
Young drunk idiot on the tram?
    City Slick the motherfucker.

That night we went to a bar,
Got drunk, and told each other
To "City Slick" every prick
In the room.

The Heart That Beats

Eventually, the people at our table
Grew curious.
"What the hell does it mean to 'City Slick' someone?"
Asked a guy with skinny arms and a beard.
I looked at Bert and flashed
my teeth. "Well," I said,
"It's when ya strip off a guy's clothes,
Hogtie his cock to a fence post,
And rape his bare-naked ass
On the plains.
Then, when ya finish,
Ya pop a cowboy hat on his head
And tell him, 'Buddy,
You've just been City Slicked.'"

The guy didn't react
But his girlfriend did.
Her face twisted up in horror
And she bolted away from the table
Never to return.

It was the high point
    of my month.

Reflections

Do you spend your nights eating popcorn and sitting in front of the tube?

Do you click off when you hear the word "thou"?

Do you have a complete inability to process anything that's going on around you

For fear that you might miss the line at KFC?

Do you like Cheese Whiz?

Scratch that

Do you like any food processed beyond the point of recognition?

Do you swamp your mind in episode after episode

Of fun-fantasy bullshit that has nothing to do with reality?

Do you worship pink-faced politicians who desperately try

Not to use the words "Nigger" and "Spic" while blatantly

Pointing the finger at people of color?

Do you adore social media? Are you one'a those geniuses

Who posts fifteen selfies a day then follows up with thirty photos

of dogs and food?

Do you believe that poetry and prose

Are a test of one's diction and not of one's honesty?

Better yet, do you read

Strictly for the purpose of entertainment?

Are you a moron?

I'll ask you again …

The Heart That Beats

Are you a moron?

Have you allowed video games to groom your mind
Into violence, so now you think picking up a gun is all
the rave? Are you okay
with a dozen superhero movies a year,
But when one comes out about the horrors of slavery,
You think it seems
"too much"?
Do you think Arabs and Persians are basically the same?
Are you of the opinion that the Middle East
Should be "dealt with" by blasting it into a big glass crater?
Do you preach liberty for all
And then have the gall to deny people their rights
To these things because who they love
in private makes you uncomfortable?
Is religion in schools your *thang*?
Do you support it just so long as the words
"Allah hu Akbar"
"Shalom Elohi"
"Hail Satan"
Are not anywhere
To be seen?

Do you hate women because they make you feel
Small? Are you that guy at the bar
Who hits on them repeatedly and then gets
mad when they don't all bow down and suck

your cock? Moreover, do you preach
Respect and equality for women
In public, and then snarl
"Bitch," "whore," and "cunt" when you are
all alone?

Are you a moron?
I'll ask you again, Johann,
Are you a moron?

The Right Thing

I asked my old college roomie, Roy,
    As I sat on his fluffy bed,
How many women
He'd been with over the years.
He came out of the bathroom still
flossing his teeth. "I don't know,"
he said. "Two hundred?"
Compared to my seventy
This seemed huge. I told him so
and he laughed. "It's really not
that big of a deal," he said. "Bullshit," I replied,
"I have to work my ass off to get pussy, and you just pluck it up like
grapes."
"Well," he said, laughing, "those days are winding down. I mean,
Tess is moving in
before she delivers."
"God, that sucks," I said. "Not really.
I know Tess isn't a super model or anything, but she's a nurse
and she can cook, and she totally loves me. I'm glad
it was her that I knocked up, even if it was by accident. I mean,
can you imagine if it had been one of those other crazy bitches I
was fucking?"
"Yeah, I guess."
"Seriously. Those girls had scorpions
in their hearts. Getting one of them pregnant woulda driven me

to suicide. And I know I freaked out a little when Tess told me the
news, but deep down
I felt peace.
And that's how I knew the right thing
was happening to me with the right person."

Roy went back into the bathroom
And flipped on the faucet.
I sat there with my hands folded, I thought
of the abortion that had killed
my last relationship, I thought
of my beautiful solitude and my writing,
The road was clear for me,
It was clear for Roy, too.

Friends

I lay with a head full of wine
in my sister's guestroom.
We'd just watched a film
About men who fled
from a Siberian gulag
And tried to walk to India.
Many died horrible deaths.
This struck my sister deep.

In the wee hours of the night,
My sister entered the room,
She sat at the desk and looked at me,
"Are you afraid of dying painfully?"
"Of course," I answered.
"What about just dying?" she asked,
"Are you afraid of death?"
"No."
She stared at me.
"Because," I explained. "It happens to everyone."
"I see people die every day. I'm a doctor. But it doesn't matter.
I'm still afraid of it."
"You shouldn't be."
"Why not?"
"Because Death can be your friend."
"How?"

"Lemme put it this way," I said, scratching my head.

"My bag is writing. But I need pressure

to push all that crazy shit out. Death is that pressure. If I didn't have

him hanging on my neck like a big ol' clock,

I'd prolly sit around all day fiddling

with my pubes because I'd have forever to do things with.

This wouldn't be a real life. So, in a way, Death makes my life

worth a damn." "Yeah, but what about when you go?

I mean, you'll just be gone. Doesn't that scare you?"

"No, because it's not really true. I'll have left

my words behind.

And that's more 'me' than anything. Plus, I'll be taking the last trip

there is with the one dude who's been with me the whole way. Now,

how can that be bad?"

My sister pondered this for a moment.

Then she got up and gave me a hug.

"Thanks Johann," she said.

"Anytime, Hannah."

Gangster in the Walls

Last night, I was looking
At old photos of my grandfather and, my God,
Was he handsome, he looked like a Brooklyn gangster
in his blue suit, and his black hair
and leather shoes glistened like wet licorice.
My grandmother, who sat next to me,
Said he was a powerhouse
And her other photos proved just that.
He flexed his muscles in the forest
And lifted slabs of concrete.
She told me he was a Juarez bootlegger
And that – when he drank – he'd turn meaner
Than a green wolverine.
She said he once threw an iron and split
her forehead in two.
She said he once ripped
An entire cabinet off the wall.
Smashed it to splinters.
I was stunned.
And, as the stories and the photos flew, my grandfather
dusted himself from oblivion and crawled
Into the walls around us.

As we sat,
Cradled in his presence,

Hans Joseph Fellmann

It was hard to believe that such a man
could be reduced
to the jittering sack of bones
that I watched die in the hospital
Four years back.
It was even harder to believe that,
Despite our feelings and memories,
He was
Gone.

FISH HARD

One July morning, my dad and I went fishing off the coast of
Berkeley,
After boarding and setting out our poles, we realized:
We were the only newbies.
The fisherman around us were all cockeyed vets,
Gnarled by the sea.
They wore rubber boots and had frizzy hair.
They smoked Marlboros
With mouths
Like anuses.
Among them, one stood out
He had skin like a crumpled paper bag,
And silver eyes
Set deep into a face with a bitten-away
Left cheek.
Tattooed across his knuckles
Were the words
FISH HARD.
And, for ten straight hours,
That's precisely what homeboy did,
As the boat rocked,
And the wind blew,
And the waves splashed
The deck.

Hans Joseph Fellmann

The captain divvied up the catch at the end of the day,
And while the other fishermen boasted
About the size of their share and held up
long proof for the camera,
Fish Hard quietly grabbed the biggest bundle
And left.

Three Weeks

I told my mother to be strong
And that I loved her,
She told me the same
And we hung up.
I left my flat
And grabbed the tram to work,
As it clicked down the tracks
I looked out the window
At Prague's pink and white sky
And orange and red trees
And verdigris spires
Encrusted with soot.
I arrived at my stop
And got off,
I went in the concrete block
With glass doors
My language school,
I said hi to the receptionist and
Knocked on my boss's open door,
She waved me in with a smile,
"Wot can I do for you, Mr. Felmanstien?" she asked
I sat in the chair across from her
And folded my hands,
"I need three weeks off," I said. "At Christmas."
She crossed her legs and gave me a dirty look,

"Why so much?" she asked

"Because," I replied, trying not to get choked up

"My granny is old and my mother

has cancer."

Her face went flush and her blue eyes sparkled,

"Then why don't you just to leave Prague

and go back home?"

Wot's keeping you here?"

I looked down at my hands,

"My writing,"

"Your writing? Can't you do it back home?"

"Sure. But I can't earn a dime in the meantime."

She bit her lip,

"Wot it feels like?" she asked,

"What's what feel like?"

"To have something that grab you like that?"

I thought of my aging grandmother

And her half-addled brain,

Of the lump in my mother's throat

And the scalpel that might remove it,

I thought of the Christmas tree, the fireplace, the stockings,

Of opening gifts with my family

And toasting with brandy over honied ham,

I knew my answer had to be worth a damn,

I sucked in deep and look my boss in the eyes,

"Well, in my brain, there's this seed, see?

And it often lies dormant,

The Heart That Beats

But when boredom swings
    Its heavy pendulum,
Or alcohol sneezes
    Its bright fire,
This seed splits and sprouts
Upward in long jellied tentacles
That crawl through my skull,
And wrap around my eyes, mouth,
And limbs
As I become a conduit for the cackling
Of the universe and spin
Like a crystal
Through space."

My boss looked at me sidelong and nodded,
"You're right," she said. "You do need three weeks."

Janis

"The Ugliest Man in High School,"
Her classmates called her.
It's true, she wasn't the standard beauty,
That skinny, orange, blonde
We see polluting the pages of
Vogue.

SHE STOOD OUT

Her shaggy hair, her pockmarked face.
She had a hunched back and when she grinned
Her yellow teeth
Connected
Her shoulders.

She couldn't flirt and wore no makeup
But put a mic in front of her
And she could
Bake your blood
And shake concrete into dust.

The first time I heard her sing
I felt terrible
For this gifted woman
Who just wanted a man

The Heart That Beats

To love her.
I wished I'd have been alive
When she was.
Then I'd have had a chance
To catch her
Before she drove that needle
Up her vein.
Maybe I'd have loved her
Maybe I'd have married her
But, as I listened to her sing,
I wondered if I would have
Ruined her.

As an outcast,
Her voice crackled
With the souls of the lonely.

As a housewife,
It may have barely carried
A single note.

Crooked Legs and Filthy Veins

Those pin-headed stiffs
With clean systems
And soft steps.
I'll never understand
People who don't
Drink. Never will they
Know the joy of crooked legs and filthy veins.
Of screaming at the moon
With a bottle in one hand
And the other balled into a fist.
Of fucking a stranger
Down the neck
With a purple
Smile.
Of busting the teeth
From an asshole's gums
With the butt of a shot-glass.
Of watching the steam rise
From their piss as it splatters
Against a cop car.
Those withering teetotalers,
Those deflated saps,
Never will they taste the sweetness
Of lewd songs at 4 a.m.,

The Heart That Beats

Of wine-drenched scrambled eggs

Chewed under

Bloodshot eyes

Better and Better

I have a Czech student
An eternal optimist.
Sometimes this annoys me.
He's constantly trying
To convince me
That we all have the power
To make our lives
"Better and better."
He'll quote some
Self-help guru called "Moses Dickballs"
(Or whatever) And say something like:
"Universe is based on 'Laws of Amazing Attraction,'
If you maintain right attitude
Everything will go perfect."

I usually bring up
Starving babies in Ethiopia
Or war-stricken children
In Iraq. "Did they not follow
the 'Laws of Amazing Attraction'?"

My student always answers the same.
"Yes, I know some people have harder lives.
But they could be more positive."
This is true.

The Heart That Beats

All of us *could*.
But what's the use
Of a smile
If a bomb
Is going to fall
On your head
Anyway.

Mother Cabrini

It was raining when
My mother and I drove
Into the Walmart parking lot,
Plastic wreaths sagged
From the streetlamps
And dead Christmas trees
Were heaped in front of the dumpsters
Like the skeletons of burned witches.
I read the last line of a poem entitled
"Christmas Eve" by Anna Sexton,
Then I closed the book and looked at my mother,
"Well," I said, "What did ya think?"
She swerved into a spot and clicked off the engine,
"I liked it," she sighed. "But it was really depressing."
"Yeah, but her words are fucking gorgeous," I replied.
"I mean, she was able to take all the depression in her life
And turn it into beauty. She even did it in death."
"What do you mean?" my mother asked.
"I mean, when she decided to off herself at forty-five,
She didn't just put a gun to her head and pull the trigger.
She got piss drunk, put on her dead mother's fur coat,
Poured herself one last glass of vodka, ran a hose from
The tailpipe of her car to the driver's side window, got in,
Cranked the engine, downed the vodka, and went out like a G."
I was screaming with my fists in the air. My mother gasped.

The Heart That Beats

"That's terrible," she cried.
"No, it's brilliant," I retorted.

A man in a white minivan
Pulled into the space in front of us,
He got out, went around to the back
And opened the trunk. He reached in
And pulled out a long sad Christmas tree,
Its branches were twisted in every direction
Like the broken arms of orphans seeking alms
And little bits of tinsel glinted from their tips like change,
He dragged it across the parking lot,
Its twigs scratching on the asphalt,
When he arrived at the dumpsters,
He lined the tree up with its dead relatives
And yanked it into the pile,
As he walked away, he took a call on his cellphone,
I looked over at my mother,
"Most people go out like that tree," I remarked.
She crinkled her eyebrows and shook her head,
"Not if they're loved," she said.

Analise

I feel so sad that you're only a poem,
I wish I could hold you in my arms,
Daddy was a coward. Mommy too.
We were selfish and didn't love you.
And now I sit here,
With tears running down my cheeks,
Screaming silently at the floor,
While I think of all you could have been.
All you could have meant to me.
How you could have filled my heart
Like warm tea,
I never gave you a chance.

My God
It's ripping the skin from my hands
And I can see your face
Through the bones.

I'm sorry
So sorry
I'm so sorry, sweet pea.

Ms. Tuesday

That six-foot dame with the sculpted ass
And the moonstone skin
And the butterscotch braid I see every Tuesday
On the nine. I try to make eye-contact,
But she always looks away,
I try to get close and, on the rare occasion she lets me
I lift my chin and inhale the flowers from her neck.
I'd like to take her out for steak and buy her earrings,
I'd like to bring her back for whiskeys and lay her on my sheets
    Run my finger up her spine,
    Choke her till her face turns red
    And her eyes light up like
    Pools of green algae.

She's the reason my ride home is holy
The goddess of my tram cabin, if you will
But barring the lust, my good mind knows
She's probably
A terrible bore.

Breakfast of Heads

If you listen to any of them, you're done.
If you take one kind word,
Or one evil word,
And sew it into your heart,
You might as well cut
The fucker out
And toss it in the trash.

Never, ever, ever listen
To them, the skulls of defeat,
The cackling hands of waste,
Keep your compass close
And your arrogance dear.
Sever the poison finger of opinion
If it ever comes near.

If you do, if you willingly brave the jagged staircase
To hell, there'll be a breakfast of heads
Waiting
For you.

ATM

I parked in front of the bank
And went to the ATM.
As I tapped at the buttons,
A woman at the adjacent machine
Panicked. I looked over and saw a bee
Buzzing loops around her arms,
She swatted it away,
Again and again,
Until finally, it scattered.
She fixed her violet dress and turned to me,
"Sorry about that," she said. "I just hate those things."
She walked off, licking her thumb
And counting her dirty wad of cash,
At that moment,
In the pot next to me,
The bee found its flower.

Miracle-Worker

My mother grew up in a big Mexican family.

They weren't poor, per se,

    Definitely working-class

And whenever a meal was on the table

She and her four brothers

Would have to eat every last bean

Lest their backsides feel the snap

Of my grandfather's belt.

The same was true if they failed

To adhere to Catholic ethics,

So, as you can imagine,

Her childhood was filled

With a lot of eating

And a lot of guilt.

When she married my father, things changed.

The man was not Catholic

    Definitely not Mexican

And the money he made as a scientist

Put our family in an economic bracket

That was easily two notches above

What my mother was used to,

This meant she had

A whole lot more dough to work with,

Of course, she spent it on food,

The Heart That Beats

And therein lay the problem,
See, she wanted to cook
Like her mother had
For a houseful of starving Mexicans
And do it in spades,
But me, my sister, and my dad
Were just two half-breeds
And a picky German,
Who snacked during the day,
My mother still cooked like she wanted to,
And naturally we couldn't eat everything
So, she had all this uneaten food
And all this resulting guilt,
What was her solution?

My mother imbued our fridge with an extraordinary power.
Anytime we didn't finish our enchiladas,
Or didn't use our salsa,
Or left sliced mangos, browning on the plate,
She just wrapped it all up in tinfoil and stuck it in.
As time passed,
Our fridge absolved the pang of waste,
In such a way, that even my father, the scientist, couldn't explain,
When that food was green with rot,
And my mother could no longer bear the stench,
She pulled it out
And dumped it
Guilt-free
In the trash.

When it Rains

I'm on a $2000 mattress and it's a Monday morning.
While a mother of three washes my balls
From her mouth, I can hear her
Boys in the next room,
Pounding, stomping, snorting.
They sound like buffalos in a craze.
I'm terrified they're going to burst
In here with baseball bats
And crack my bones.
I roll over in bed and cover my naked ass
With a sheet, homegirl comes back from the sink
And lays down next to me
"I know you're a player," she says,
"In fact, I bet you're gonna go off
With another woman tonight."
Had she said this 3
or 6
or 9
months ago, she'd have been flat out
Wrong.
But, by some miracle, I do have a date tonight,
With another woman. And by some other miracle
I even have a woman
Waiting for me
Back in Prague.

The Heart That Beats

I don't know what it is.
I don't know why they come in groups
I mean
I'll go on solo jags for months,
So long that I forget my cock is there and then,
out of the great blue sky,
2 or 3 or more
Will land in my lap
And I'll be swimming in hair and boobs and thighs,
Maybe it's the hormones. Maybe
It's the pheromones. Maybe
It's luck and the resulting confidence. Whatever it is,
Women almost always come together.

I'm not saying I haven't had one-offs;
Girls that just walk out of the night
On their own, then leave,
Never to be seen again,
But for me, it's usually
Dry, dry, dry,
Then BAM
It pours

The Fit

Sat at my computer, typing out poems
I was interrupted by a sudden blue screen.
Then, the whole machine
Shut down.
I tried to reboot.
This took some time
And, as the clock hands spun,
I felt my precious poems
Evaporating like tea steam.
I jumped up and down, crushed beer cans,
And tore the covers off my bed
Then I noticed an interesting book on my shelf
So, I took it into the next room
And plopped on a chair
And tried to read.

But every fourth word was blurred
Like a raindrop had fallen on the page
And I felt the red teeth of rage
Biting into my guts again
I flung the book against the wall
And stormed back into my room
And when I saw that my computer
Was not nearly finished
With whatever it was doing,

The Heart That Beats

I pointed at its face and screamed

"You piece of shit! I'll fucking kill you!"

Then my whole body lit up

And I beat the air with my fists

Shouting,

"You cunt!"

"You cunt!"

"You cunt!"

"You cunt!"

I could feel my tendons and muscles and brains

Fiending for me to bleed the scream outta someone.

Preferably a dainty little teen

With fake eyelashes and a stick

Up her ass. I looked around

The room and the walls were breathing and braiding

With the monsters

Of my past.

I went to my bathroom

Splashed cold water

On my cheeks

I slapped myself in the face,

When I finished, I looked up at the mirror

And saw a desperate and deranged man

A stranger, I barely knew him

But by his slanted eyes and long grin

I could tell that he knew me.

As we stared at each other

Hans Joseph Fellmann

As the seconds trickled by
I was a single tick from collapse
When suddenly, my computer rebooted
And my poems reappeared
And everything was
Okay again

Crazy Good Boy

We drove through the tall forest, up
To the A-frame cabin where I'd spent my childhood
We looked around the front yard and noticed that a few things
Had changed. The gas tank was gone,
The pine trees were clipped,
And the mountain misery was shaved
Down to the dirt.

"Remember that mountain misery?" my Dad said, pointing.
"Tommy used to romp around in that shit for hours
Before running off into the trees
To do God knows what."

Our old dog Tommy owned the forests of Sugar Pine
And when he wasn't chasing rodents or rummaging
Through the neighbors' trash, he cut rings around the lake below
Or galloped up a rock to piss off the top

"He commanded this place," my Dad said,
"And he was such a good dog."

It was true,
Tommy was a good dog,
Even though the pit in his blood
Made him crazy.

Hans Joseph Fellmann

I remember my fifth birthday,

When my dad surprised me

By opening the garage door and letting

Baby Tommy bolt into my arms.

After that, he pretty much became *my* dog

Which is why when I think of him now, it hurts.

See, it was me that night

(A decade later)

Who left the gate open,

And Tommy, being the crazy good boy

That he was, figured it was okay

And ran out after

The moon

For three days, we could not find a trace

Until we phoned some clinic

One town over. We were told

Tommy had been found

In the street

Without a collar

By the time we got there,

He had been in the freezer for 48 hours

When they brought him out

He was curled into a little ball

He glistened under the fluorescent lights

I remember touching his ear,

The Heart That Beats

Velvety soft, like always
But stiff and cold

Now there's an urn on my Dad's work desk,
But I like to think of Tommy out there in the forests,
Scaring off the chipmunks and proudly
Biting up the earth.

Mountain Girl

We pulled alongside her at an intersection
She drove a dented-up Chevy with balding tires
And letters scratched from its logo so it read
"HE Y"
As we waited for the light,
I watched her through the window,
She wore her hair in a bun
Under a netted fishing hat,
Her oval face was crusted with dirt
But still pretty
A cigarette let up curly-cues of smoke
She lifted it to her lips
Took a long drag
And when the light clicked green
She leaned her dirty pretty face
Out the window
And spat.
My mother wrinkled her nose,
"What a pig"
The girl cocked a half-smile and drove off,
I wished I were in that truck
With her

Nickle-Sized Hole

Two hours on the fishing boat and already I was ill
I'd taken some pills
And slept a little
But it didn't matter.
The sea shook my guts still
And I retched beef jerky
Into a nickel-sized hole.
When I stopped and sat down,
A large black man in a beanie
Grinned at me with lightning teeth
"You got that look," he said. "That sick look."
"I just vomited..." I groaned. "I'm not really
used to this."
"Take a while," he said. "I been
at this ten years n' sometime I still get sick.
But'chu know, I ain't never been
really sick. N' boy, you ain't *really* sick right now, neither."
"Oh?"
"No.
One time I was fishin' wit this dude who was so sick,
He straight jump off tha boat n' start swimmin' back'ta shore.
Dude, almost died'a hypothermia."
"Jesus," I cried.
"Anotha time, this one crazy muthafucka turn green,
N' start pukin' his lungs out, n' when the cap'n come'ta help,

Dude pull a knife on him and demand he go back'ta port.

Fool was down'ta do *time* jus' so he could feel betta."

Big Daddy kept at the stories,

I listened as long as I could

But eventually I had to go back

And puke through

That nickel-sized hole,

When I returned, I saw

Homeboy was now on deck

Reeling in a big blue cod,

I wiped the chunks from my lips

And joined him.

Ali Baba

I gulped the last of my wine and zipped up my pants.
"I'll be there in a second," I yelled,
I grabbed my coat and got in the car,
Where my parents were waiting,
My dad started the engine and off we drove,
"What's this place we're meeting them at?" I asked
"It's called 'Ali Baba,'" my mom replied,
"And it's a nice restaurant, so
let's all try
to be nice."
"Whatever."

We arrived at the restaurant an hour later,
It had a terrace with heat lamps and potted palms
And cheap metal tables painted black,
Seated at the back, my sister and her husband,
    Ramin
We joined them and our waitress gave us menus,
"Can I get you guys anything
to start off?" Ramin shifted his gut
Rolled his sleeves up his hairy forearms,
"Vee arty know vat vee vant," he said,
Listing a slew of dishes.
It didn't matter that we'd all had Persian before,
He *was* Persian, so he knew best.

Hans Joseph Fellmann

The waitress brought our food:
Grilled meats, vegetables, yogurts, salads, soups, sauces, breads.
Ramin grabbed two of everything and started in,
He had an underbite so big
He could almost place the food in the bowl of his lower jaw
Without ever opening his mouth.

As he smacked his lips and grunted and bounced
His stupid bushy eyebrows with pleasure,
I thought of all the things he'd done to piss me off:
    Horning in on my sister's trip to visit me in Prague,
    Making my sister cry on their wedding day,
    Starting fights with me and my friends unnecessarily,
    Quitting his job and letting my sister foot the bill for everything,
    Lounging in his boxers all day, eating cereal and watching porn,
    Never giving my sister kids or even entertaining the idea,
    Being a general douchebag and a moron
    to boot.

When I finished my thought bubble, half the food was gone.
I ate a skewer of meat and a zucchini slice and Ramin ate the rest,
He lay his hands on his gut and burped softly,
My sister patted his wave of thinning hair and grinned,
What the fuck does she see in him? I thought
The waitress came by and asked if we'd have dessert,
"Oh yes," Ramin said, sitting up.
Another list:
Puffed pastries, pistachio parfait, rose water ice cream, almond cake,

The Heart That Beats

The waitress brought everything out
And set it in front of his drooling underbite,
My sister scooped a spoonful of ice cream and lifted it to his lips,
Then it occurred to me,
Ramin was not only her husband
He was also her baby

Tough Titty

I wake up and look across my room
My curtains are slowly burning
My bed is a soft coffin
And the light from the bathroom window
Is a shaft of gold
I am living and breathing
Inside a dream
Where Death chokes my head
With a towel and says:

"What's the matter?
There's no other time
Like this
Write! Write! Write! Write!
Write! Write! Write! Write!
Write! Write! Write! Write!"

I whimper,
And in my most
Sniveling voice, I say,
"It's *haaaaard*."

Archeology

A hidden vein,

A broken plume,

A warrior, a drunk, a buffoon

A chewer of worms, a black revolver,

A horn on the head of a heretic,

A charlatan who strains truth from his wounds,

A green mist that lingers in the space

Between your attic and your garage

An invisible hitman,

Walking down the street

In a suit of blue,

The highest shelf

Where the oldest bottles

With the oldest secrets

Reside,

A transmutation of genes,

The last candle in a cave

Burning itself beautifully

To death,

An icepick to the face

Of mediocrity

A bleeding tooth

Hans Joseph Fellmann

In the mouth
Of liar,
An elegant weed
In a bed of plastic
Flowers

A slow-growing crack
Up the neck of a
Bureaucrat

An idiot
With the reddest apple
On his palm

A hen
Scratching at the air
As her head's being
Severed

One pink tile
In a labyrinth of
White

Your aborted daughter
Holding your hand
In a dream

Your poisoned grandfather
Crunching his wrinkles to a point
Before vanishing into
His sheets.

Mediocrity

The magazine-whore
Who peddles his dainty words
For pre-show
Rimjobs

The bearded, bespectacled
Hipster who haunts the bars,
Smoking cigars,
Spouting other people's junk

The affected man-child
Who dons tweed and sings
Platitudes into his swirling
Snifter

The milk-faced moron
With the long hair, who believes
That all the poetry he needs
Is a neat scarf

The sour old coot who sits
In silence behind his glass
So that it speaks
For him,

The wine-drunk cougar who lounges
On her terrace

All afternoon
Penning too-da-loos,

The military brat
With the chipmunk cheeks
And the purple diary full of
Sex fails

Or any one
You might find
At your local
Coffee shop

34

I woke up this morning

With a precious hangover

Eyes sour, mouth bitter

Stomach like a cement mixer

I schlepped to the shower

And let the scalding water

Melt away the grey

Then, I got dressed

In my ratty old clothes

And went to work

When the tram never came

I stood in the cold

Cursing and screaming

Between the smokers,

Who ignored me silently,

When I finally arrived

At my lesson, I took a shit

That was long and wet

And made the sound

Of bubble-wrap

Being popped

I wiped and went

To my student's office

He shook my hand

And grinned

Hans Joseph Fellmann

"I just won ten grand
For being lawyer of the year," he boasted.
I thought about the four more submission rejections
I'd received the previous day
"That's wonderful," I said.

We had our lesson and I went to my next,
It took me forty-five minutes
To get there and on the way
Some dude with scraggly white hair
Cut me off on the crosswalk
I kicked his bumper
Called him a "motherfucker"
And grabbed my crotch

When I arrived at my lesson
Tired and pissed off
My student looked at the clock
"You're late," he told me.
"Bad traffic."
"That's always your excuse."
We sat down and started our lesson,
I told him about the Foreign Police postponing
My application for permanent residency again.

"The third time in three months," I yelled.
My student laughed. "Maybe they will kick you out next time?"

The Heart That Beats

The lesson ended and I went
Again to Social Services
To pay the blimps on the top floor
Another hundred dollars
Then I went down to the basement
And grabbed another damn document
For my permanent residency

Now, I'm sat on a bus,
Contemplating my age
I'm 34 today
And all I have to show are
4 rejection letters
3 birthday texts
2 swollen feet
And a head full of angst.

Americans

I can always spot the Americans in the streets of Prague,
Their baggy clothes, their unlaced shoes
Their lopsided backpacks filled to the point
Of splitting. Their fat, ugly faces
Fixed with the same expression
As brainless guppies.

They travel in loud oblivious packs, wandering the city
In search of the wildest bar, the tightest club,
They talk about their lives back home
And the crap they did the night before
About their absolute *favorite* places
For burritos, burgers, and Vietnamese
They stink of beer, body spray, and cheese,
They blab on speakerphones in public
And always lose their wallets and keys,
They're a disgusting, moronic breed
They make me want
To puke
Right down
My shirt

Pennywise

I laugh so hard I get sick,
Deep down, where the folds of my stomach
Turn and the food decays
And the arms of little animals
Reach up for
The sun

I laugh so hard I break
Things, like tables and chairs
And seams on my jacket
Not even the ceilings are safe

I laugh so hard I bend
Not just time or space,
But my earth-quaking gut
Like the wind that bends
A penny

I laugh so hard I imagine
things, like a cat
being indignantly shaved or
A clown popping out a urethra or
A puckered anus being painted with a mustache

I laugh so hard I make
Bums laugh, crazy drunken ones,
Who cling to building sides like scabs

Hans Joseph Fellmann

I laugh so hard I die
In the molecules of my cells,
An explosion of tiny howling mouths,
Fizzing up from my
Slack-jawed carcass,

I laugh so hard
    I laugh so hard

Even when the joke's not funny
And everyone's asleep
But me

Watching

I sit on this bench in sad delirium,

Watching as the paper gulls circle

Over the black river

The trams crawl by like giant metal caterpillars

The clouds move overhead, opening and closing

    Eyes of sharp blue

A toothless child

Points at the trash and laughs,

Points at me and laughs,

Points at the castle and asks

    Dada, do the ravens make nests

    In the spires

I sit here in my churning gloom,

Cold, unnerved, frustrated,

As the pencils sketch a prison

Around me

As the trees stand like

A rash of fried skeletons

As the party boats

Lay dead on the Vltava

Like discarded

Red cups

As I imagine that somewhere,

Behind some curtained window,

Hans Joseph Fellmann

A little girl's hand is crushed
By her rapist's boot

I waste away here
In the shadow of Granddaddy clock
As he cackles and blinks his wicked
Numbers in my face
And the gong of his belly
Shakes my skin

I am a snail eclipsed by tar
A night-crawler knotted
At the end of a hook
And as I sail out to sea on this deadly string
I know that the patina of life has no memory
And the maw of history has
No book

776 752 214

I'm a miserable person
I really, really am

I don't like being near
Other people
And when I'm forced
To talk to them
I often think of
Plucking their eyes out
With a fork

I spend most of my time
Alone
Clicking words onto a page
Or pickling my organs
In booze

I hate children
Especially little boys
And when I hear them
Bickering or fighting
I get nostalgic for
Meat-grinders

I'm a cheater
A thief

Hans Joseph Fellmann

A liar
A racist, to be sure
But as my gene pool is more splotched
Than an incontinent toddler's underwear
It's really just me hating myself

I don't care much for women
But I despise men
So I guess in some way
You could call me
A feminist

I used to murder animals as a kid,
But, now that I'm grown
I take great pleasure
In buying my animals pre-murdered
And packaged

I once made a girl
Drink my cum
From a shot glass,
And then I made her lick
Her shit from my cock

I'd certainly be a serial-killer
If I could
But I'm a lazy motherfucker
So, the temptation to watch movies

The Heart That Beats

And get drunk alone

In my bedroom

Outweighs the urges

I have when I see a short skirt

Stretched around a pair of

Long, beautiful

Legs,

Welp,

That pretty much

Sums me up

Shoot me an email sometime

Or hit me on my cell

You've already got my number

My Best Friend

My best friend died

He was my hero with scary blue eyes

And white muscles and red lips

Which expelled the most horrible laugh

Nobody fucked with him

And if they did, they felt

    The crushing blow

Of his fist against their gut

My best friend was bigger and stronger and tougher

Than me and you and your best friend

    Put together

He had a rumbling heart of spring water

And courage that could split trees

But he was spoiled green

And when his mother tumbled

Down the stairs

And cracked open her skull

In front of his eyes,

He cracked open

    Too

For years, he battled

Against the maddening guilt

    Booze and dope and pills

Living in trailers on hills

And crawling through

Gutters

The Heart That Beats

Then, one winter's day
It was just too much
Alone in a cold motel room
    My best friend
Swallowed his last pill
And pierced his last vein
The paramedics found him
    Hours later
With his blue eyes rolled white
His red lips turned pale
    They tried to save him
But his muscles deflated like
Old balloons
And his rumbling heartbeat faded
    Weaker and weaker
Like footsteps down a long hall
He died shortly after
Among the Christmas lights
And the breathing tubes,
His spirit left his giant, withered body
And rose through the ceilings
    Into the night
I hadn't seen my best friend in ages
Before that night, but now
He's a regular guest,
He visits me when I laugh out loud
Or splash cold water on my face
And check the mirror

A Walk Alone in March

Love is not indestructible
It is very,
    very fragile
It can be killed
    With a little poison
    or a little force
It's easy as crushing a ladybug
    With your toe.

Coke Nail

I don't know how to do this
I've never written a love poem before
I feel like your friends hate me
I feel like they're mad 'cuz
I'm taking you away
But is it so bad
    That one of you escapes
    The doldrums
    Of a life untested?
I love you, Jennifer,
And I think I always have,
Don't be afraid to take my long-nailed hand,
You knew it was coming
After all

Your Sour Cream Heart

Let it die

Go ahead
I'm giving you my permission,
The next time it swells up
And scratches at the
Back of your ear
Just stir your pasta in the pan
Or pick up the phone
Hell,
Do both

The next time you're in your bed
Staring at the yellow eyes of the night
And you feel it slowly unfold
Down your spine
Brush it off
Take a shoehorn to it
Fuck,
A flamethrower

Let it die
Or, better yet
Kill it dead
Over dinner conversations

The Heart That Beats

And great wine
While screwing fabulously
Or holding hands
Just fling it off the fucking cliff, screaming
And fuggedaboutit

I mean, why not?
Your uncle with the body shop
Did,
And your aunt with the hair salon
Did,
And your father, the mailman,
And your mother, the seamstress,
And your sister with the solid gold voice
Who sells baby diapers wholesale,
Be like them and say "Fuck it"
Too
It ain't but a little bitty ol' thang
That the Devil slipped in
Your drink,
Anyhoo,

Screw your sour cream heart!
Or even an hour of any of your days
Just make it into your tiny pet
That you pat on the head
While blowing the steam
From your mint tea

Hans Joseph Fellmann

And if it ever grows behind your back
Like a wall of ivy
Never let it take you over
Never let it seize your veins
    Or your eyes or your brains or your guts,
Never let it yank you from your chair
And lift you into the sky
Like the proudest star
Never let it own you, consume you,
    Envelope you, swallow you
Never let it stalk you
On the reddest midnight
When the fireflies swarm
Your shakily held lantern of a moon
Never let it give you that,
Take that from you,
Never

Missed Call

I keep my room very neat
That way, whenever I disturb something,
There's always a trail.
Right now, my desk is covered
In wads of snotty tissues
My bed is a crumpled mess
And my clothes are all over the floor
My computer hisses like
A busted furnace
And my bookcase is toppled
With books spilling out
Like guts from a shamed samurai
On top of the book pile
Lies a collection of love poems
By my favorite poet,
Its spine is wrinkled
And its pages are sprinkled
With dark dots

FUCK

It's the night before she arrives
And I'm in my bed with my blanky
Up to my chin and my eyes sealed tight
Every conversation we've ever had
Is flashing through my mind
I can barely breathe
I can barely *breathe*
Jesus, that flat patch of pixels
I fell in love with
Is on a plane soaring towards me
In a few hours
She'll land and pop into three dimensions
And kiss me with *real red lips*
Holy shit
What have I gotten myself into?
This was never supposed to be *real,*
Just images and thoughts and dreams and plans
Not an actual living, breathing, eating, farting, fucking person
In my midst
Jesus Christ's speckled clown balls!
I've really gone and done it now
Is this a mistake? Have I fucked myself
For eternity? Have I fucked her?
I'm *going to* fuck her, I'm gonna fuck her
So good that her little pink toenails are gonna

The Heart That Beats

Pop off whistling
Shit!
I feel like a gremlin's
Pouring lighter fluid
Into my
Veins
My heart is a flaming apple
My eyes are cracked-out mice
Spinning around and around in their wheels
There is no form to anything
The universe is a bucket of shredded cabbage
On my head,
Fuck! Fuck! Fuck! Fuck! Fuck! Fuck! Fuck!
This is nails-through-the-cheeks *crazy*,
This is twelve screaming dicks slammed up the keister *insane*
What have I done, girl?
What have *we* done?
I guess your cousin is proud of himself,
Perched up there on his cloud of smoke
Laughing his Crazy Horse laugh
His muscly arms folded
Watching us with eyes so blue
They should have tropical fish
Swimming in them
Fuck!
I need to keep yelling,
Fuck!
Okay,

Okay,

My forearm is starting to hurt

And this is becoming

Unproductive

But

Fuck

Climax

Cables snapping,
Grand pianos falling from the clouds
And crashing into rivers
Of blueberries

Bullfrogs
Chewing down rainbows
Then burping up
Iridescent bubbles

Homunculus
With a jeweled clock on his back
That wilts a flower
With every tick

Two porcelain hands
Slowly lifting your head
From your neck,
Leaving your eyeballs
Floating in space

The violet lips
Of a siren
Blowing away the petals
Of your dried dandelion
Spine

Hans Joseph Fellmann

A sword slicing open
Your belly
And the wound breaking into
Laughter

All the cats
In the ivied cemetery
Feeding on the same screaming
Mouse

Hooves thumping
Down a spiral
Staircase

Fingers spidering
Across an infant's
Window

Then,
Without warning,

An orchestra
In a cathedral of the damned,
Where your nerves are the strings on the violins,
And your guts are the pipes on the oboes,
And your teeth, the cymbals,
And your testicles, the drums,
And your cock, the great fluted organ,

The Heart That Beats

Blasting out the top

Of your jagged, black-skinned

Roof

Chainsaw Lover

I was always under the impression
  That love made a man
  Non-violent
That when his heart finally found
A woman it settled
Like a fat hillbilly
Into a bubbling Jacuzzi
Then, any trace of violence
Instantly withered
Into the dark recesses
From whence it sprang

This may be true for some men,
But for me, love has not erased my violence
Rather heightened it, to the point that
If a man so much as whistles
At my new girlfriend
My first thought is not to push
Or even to kick
But to march up to him
With a spoon and a bit of rope
And tie him to the nearest bench
And dismember him
With slow strokes
Of dull metal

The Heart That Beats

My new girlfriend finds
This impulse of mine
Very unattractive,
Yet it is her love
That inspired it
In the first place
For her sake, I try to control it
And when I do
She loves me more
Then we go for a walk
And another guy whistles,
Only now
I'm patting my breast pockets
For a chainsaw

Whipped

My buddy Toby threw a BBQ
At his flat in Žižkov this weekend
He set up chairs and tables and couches
On his top-floor balcony and grilled
Chicken and sausages in his "Kiss the Chef" apron
The sun flashed in the sky like a new dime
And we tanned our necks
And drained our beers
And bullshitted
As the music played
And the tower shined above the rooftops
Like a big metal middle finger

When the food was ready, there was a knock at the door
Toby ran down and returned
With two beautiful women, a blonde and a brunette
Toby gave the blonde a kiss, the brunette a hug
I said hi to the blonde and leaned
Into the brunette, I could smell
Apples in her curls
We shook hands
And went out on the balcony
Where I filled my plate
And sat down and
The brunette sat down beside me

The Heart That Beats

Crossing her legs and swishing
Her hair in the sunshine
Till I was covered
In flecks of light

My cock was so hard and sharp
I could have pushed it through
A block of cheese
I felt my girlfriend watching me
Her eyes looking up at me
From my lap. I tried not to pay attention
To the sculpted bulge of
Tits and legs and ass
Just beside me
But when she took a bite of her drumstick
And licked the grease from her lips,
I about farted my guts
Through my dickhole
I started thinking about all the ways
My girl had done me wrong
    How she'd been neglecting me lately
    Because of her new job
    And how she just didn't talk to me
    Like a lady
I downed another beer
Then another and another
I cracked jokes at Mrs. Thang
And she whipped her mouth open

And laughed. I was the funniest guy
In the room, I knew I had it in the bag
This made me smile
But before she could
Give me her digits,
Or flip me upside down
With her jiggly hips
I dabbed the corners
Of my mouth with a napkin
And went home to call
My girl

Juan

He's always there

He's always,
Always,
There

He walks with me
    When I walk,
He sleeps with me
    When I sleep,
He talks with me
    When I talk,
He moves like a rat
Through grease as I chat
With my folks or woo
A lady or step in a puddle
And see his rippling face
Staring back at me

He is the grit in my hair
The grey skin beneath
My long fingernail
I hear him in my pillow
When I lay my ear down
I smell him in my erection

Hans Joseph Fellmann

When a woman spreads her legs,

He is unwashed and insane;

The clapping of a satyr's hooves

Against the street,

I know him and I feel him,

And when the cunts

Spit their forked tongues at me,

He transforms my fist

Into a blade

Moondust

It's a hot night in June
The tram is whistling by my window
And the drunks outside
Are cuttin' up a tune

A good film colors my screen
And a cold glass of something nice
Is resting in my hand
Like the head of a dog

It's my last night to be free
My final scare with the ghosts
Before the moon dissolves at my fingertips
And the pretty girl I love
Jumps in this whirlpool
With me

Long Diamonds

I can't do this anymore
I can't DO this anymore!
NOT anymore,
Not one second
Of ANY of
It
The folding,
The packing,
The clothes;
Neat squares ready to slip
On my back
And block the sun
As I run through the fields,
And the trees,
Past faces and houses and mountains,
As the tears stream back from my eyes
Like long diamonds
And my sad heart
Empties,

I can't do this anymore,
THIS!
The calls,
The flights,
The wondering,

The Heart That Beats

As another family member
Dies,
As another friend
Drinks a bottle
Of pills,

I can't do this anymore!
The death,
The rot,
The bones of my feet,
Rattling in my boots
As I christen a new land,

ABSOULTELY NOT!
NO!
FORGET IT!
YOU WON'T TAKE ME!

You sweet woman,
YOU EVIL SHOELACE OF SNOT!

NO!
NOPE!

Stay there on the moon,
Stay there in your crater,
Don't lift me by the chin
With your curled finger

And kiss me on the lips,

That my heart become a flowerbed

For the damned,

And my eyes, swirling vortexes

Of gems,

YOU BITCH!

YOU WHORE!

NO!

No

no

Thank you

Ex Nihilo

After being holed up
In my room for days on end
Drinking, shitting, crying
And trying to force words through
Fingers like dry French fries
I decided to take
A walk

I grabbed a small water bottle
And slipped on my thongs,
I walked outside
Into the sun

The manicured houses in my parents' new neighborhood
All had gumdrop trees and conical hedges
And little iron fences with roses poking
Through

Around them, the nature seemed plastic
The oaks grew like fat mannequin arms
And the butterflies seesawed
Through the air, as if on strings

I walked for miles
Till I came to a freeway, flowing with cars
There were signs everywhere

Hans Joseph Fellmann

No Left Turn
No Right Turn
No U Turn
No Exit

I picked a nearby tree
And plopped myself in its shade
Watching the cars race past my toes

As I sat there sipping water
Every third driver craned his neck
To see me. I started to feel
Like I had a second head
Sprouting from my
Shoulder

I imagined a squad car pulling up
Two cops step out
One woman, One man
The female cop approaches
With her thumb on her gun
Asks me what I'm doing
"Nothing," I say
"Do you live around here?' she asks
"Not really"
"Have you been drinking?"
"Yes"
She notices my water

The Heart That Beats

And tells me not to
Get smart
I tell her it is too late
Before I know, I am in the back of the squad car
With a black eye and handcuffs choking
My wrists
They throw me in a cell
With the drunks and the lunatics,
My father has to come
To bail me out
On the way home he asks me
What the fuck had happened,
"Nothing," I say.

The word rang out in my mind. I snapped from my
Dream and stood up. I felt the makings
Of something juicy brewing. I walked back home,
Sat at my computer
And typed.

Pass the Pepper

You bring his hair into our bed,
You put his smile on our mirror,
You wash his breath off in our shower,
You push his skin out in our toilet,
When you rinse your mouth, he spills
Into our sink
When you paint your nails
His laughter fills my ears
You slip on a dress for me
And all I see is him

    Your eyes are stamps that he's licked
    Your tits are his spider-veined pillows
    Your legs are the churners of his dreams
    Your heels are the soft butter cubes on his table
    Your face is the street where his car accident happens
    Your nipples are two rusty pennies in his pocket
    Your hair is made of the smoke from his cigarettes

I go to hold you but my fingers
Touch his fingerprints
I try to kiss you but
I only taste his seed,
You're the reason men
Murder after dinner
Now, pass the pepper
Please

Thirtysomethings

At around two, I showed up
At my buddy Devon's
He greeted me
With a hug. We went out on his balcony
Where the San Diego sun
Burned down upon us
We stoked the coals on the tobacco
And passed the hookah hose around

"How's it going?" I asked.
Devon opened his mouth
And blew out a freight train
Then he tossed me the hose
And reclined
"Shitty," he said.

"Wanna talk about it?"
"Nothing to tell, really. I mean, my ex-wife's
A whore who ran off with a man
Who used to beat her in high school.
Plus, she's trying to take our son away.
To top it all off, she's five-months pregnant,
And we don't even know
Who the father is."
I thought about my recent breakup,
Suddenly, getting dumped by

A 35-year-old Californian ditz
Who got cold feet
Before moving to Prague
    Didn't seem so bad
I took a hit and passed it to Devon,
He sucked at the nozzle and blew snakes
Out his nose

"Well, have you been seeing anyone lately?" I asked.
"Kinda," he said. "I did a few Tinder dates.
All with thirtysomethings."
"How'd those go?"
"Let's see, the first girl had a pretty face
But I made the mistake of trusting that
It matched her body. When we met at a bar, I saw
She was 250 lbs. of pure cauliflower
Plus, she had a toe that was ready to rot off her foot."
"Jesus," I cried
"And then I went out with this one blonde
Who was really cute, but she had this vial
Of grey stuff around her neck
And when I asked her what it was, she said,
'Oh, these are my dead father's ashes,
We were really close.'
So anyways, that ended that,"
"My God."
"And then the last date
Was with this brunette girl, sweet as pie

The Heart That Beats

But completely deaf
And I don't know how to sign
So, we spent the entire date
Pointing at things and smiling
Eventually, I just pointed to my phone
And mouthed the words
'I gotta go.'"

I laughed so hard
I almost choked
Devon just sat there
With a scowl
"It's not funny, Johann," he said.
"Shit's tough out there,
And you and I aren't getting
Any younger."

A group of teenage girls
In bikinis walked by,
I whistled at one and she waved,
I looked over at Devon
And winked
"No, but they are," I said.

Under My Damn Blanket

Last night, I was drunk and I picked up
The phone. I called her, which was
A stupid thing to do,
But I couldn't help myself
We were supposed to spend the summer together
Supposed to move to Europe together
But pride and greed and death and bullshit
Got in the way and now
Here it is, my last day
And I called her and
She's coming over
Fuck, what do I do?
I was ready to leave
I was ready to hop on that fucking plane
And say too-da-loo to this miserable country
I even had a song telling her to piss-off
All picked out for Facebook and everything
But now she's coming over
    She's coming over!
And I'm in my room right now
With a stinking mouth
And a crusty face
And an aching body
And an even more aching heart
And she's on her way

The Heart That Beats

I can hear her shoe-heels clicking up the steps
I can picture her red-nailed finger pressing the doorbell
I can sense her moving towards my room
I can taste all of her
    Her eyes, her mouth, her lips, her teeth,
        Her ears, her tits, her legs, her arms, her cunt
One big ball of strawberries and rot
Fuck
This is a goddamn horror
Flick. What am I going to say?
What am I going to do?
Here ... under my damn blanket
Shivering and guarding
My heart with both hands
    (as if that'll do any good)
I've really opened the fucking bag on this one
I've really screwed the pooch up its ass with both socks on
What if she's slept with someone already?
I know I have, I fucked
Some girl in my buddy's shower and came
All over her shoulder
Jesus
What have I done?
I'm asking the fan right now but it's not answering,
Maybe I'll ask the chair?
The couch?
The cat?

Hans Joseph Fellmann

The moon?
The stars?
Fuck you, guys, why
Won't you answer me?

Monkey

So, she came
And the world didn't explode
And the planets didn't misalign
The sun kept burning
The moon hung up there in its shittin' basket

See, I opened the door,
    And I hugged her,
    And I kissed her,
    And I fucked her
And now she's laying asleep in my bed
My dick is covered in her blood
My face is covered in her spit
Our guts are both filled with good wine
And I've told her,
    I've told her
That I love her
And that I'm ready to do what it takes
To make this work. The monkey
Is on her back now
And, if she flicks it off,
The devil won't be paying *me*
A visit

5A

I arrived at the airport with all my luggage
And a face full of grief
The woman I loved
Had just hooked her index fingers
Into my tear ducts and ripped them
Into small waterfalls
I walked up to the counter
And gave the lady my details
She crinkled her eyebrows
"Passport please," she said
I gave her my passport
Then she weighed my bags
"You're over," she said. "But it's okay."
"Thank you," I sighed, as she handed me
My boarding pass. I was in a middle seat,
"Is there any way you can get me an aisle?"
She shrugged and clicked into her computer
"Go through security and see me at the gate."
I gathered my things and said goodbye
To my folks. Jennifer, now my ex, called my cell,
"Have a safe flight," she said,
"Thanks," I managed

I went through security,
    Waving at my folks the whole way

The Heart That Beats

I collected my crap
    And went to the gate,
The woman who'd checked me in
    Was waiting there
She handed me a new pass
"Enjoy your flight," she said, smiling,
"5A," I read aloud, "First Class,
Holy
shit"

The ticket agent led me
Into the tiny line
For first class
I stepped on the plane and
Through the red curtain and my seat
    was twice the size of anything in the rear
I had my own personal cubby,
    A packaged blanket and pillow,
    A clothes hanger, a widescreen,
    And ample legroom
I decided I'd skip the valium
    A cousin's departing gift
Then, as I reclined in my seat
A woman on the intercom asked
    "Will Monsieur Felmanstien,
    Please come to the front entrance?"
I got up and walked there, smiling
    Maybe they want me to meet the captain?

Hans Joseph Fellmann

I heard yelling in French, a fat woman
In glasses, barking furiously at her staff
"May we see your boarding pass?"
A stewardess asked. I shrugged
"Sure"
She looked at it
    Clucked,
"We gave you the wrong one, sir"
She handed me another
    I looked at the seat number
    Coach
"Fuck," I mumbled

I gathered my things
Wearing a terribly sad face,
But as I walked towards coach
There was one more stop
"Your seat is here, sir," a woman said, touching my arm
She showed me an aisle seat
In business, I smiled
    Thanked her
My heart thanked
    Her too

Free Bird

Nobody does it right, nobody even
    comes close
Everyone fucks it up, everyone tears the heart
    from another's chest
    And dropkicks it
    Into the dumpster,
It is the way of things,
And it will always be
The way of things
Even when our cars fly
    And our buildings float
    And our brains are small humming computers
Love, my friend, knows no rule
And the man who tries to trap it
With wires
Or money
Or time
Or anger
Is the world's greatest fool